Living

Spaces

Over 30 instant room transformations

Living Spaces

Over 30 instant room transformations

Stewart & Sally Walton

LORENZ BOOKS

First published in 2000 by Lorenz Books

© Anness Publishing Limited 2000

Lorenz Books is an imprint of
Anness Publishing Limited
Hermes House, 88–89 Blackfriars Road, London SE1 8HA

ISBN 0 7548 0310 4

A CIP catalogue record for this book is available from the British Library

Publisher: Joanna Lorenz
Senior editor: Doreen Palamartschuk
Editor: Linda Doeser
Photographers: Graham Rae, Lucinda Symons, Rodney Forte, John Freeman
Stylists: Sacha Cohen, Catherine Tully, Diana Civil, Andrea Spencer, Fanny Ward,
Leean Mackenzie, Judy Williams
Projects on pages 14-17, 20-23, 26-29 & 36-39 by Sacha Cohen
Illustrator: Madeleine David
Designer: Ian Sandom
Jacket designer: Clare Baggaley

Printed in Hong Kong/China

1 3 5 7 9 10 8 6 4 2

CONTENTS

ℐNTRODUCTION

WHETHER AN OPEN-PLAN LOFT CONVERSION, a small front room in a country cottage or a grandly proportioned sitting room in a traditional city house, your living space is a relaxing haven. Ironically, as well as being your personal space in the strongest sense of the term, it is also the most public part of your home – the place to which you invite family, friends and other guests. It is important for both of these functions that you create an atmosphere that reflects your individual personality and style.

These living space makeovers have been inspired by many different cultures and periods in history, from the wood panelling of colonial America to the sophisticated elegance of Gustavian Sweden, and from hi-tech contemporary to traditional Japanese. They include treatments for walls and floors, curtains, cushions, lamps and lampshades, but large or small, the projects have all been designed to be strong on imagination and easy on the pocket. Some makeovers require a few pieces of special equipment, but most need only basic tools and materials. The techniques covered include almost all aspects of home-making crafts, from painting to sewing. You do not have to be an expert, as there are masses of professional hints and tips for short-cuts.

By carefully planning your wall and floor treatments, soft furnishings and finishing details, you will create a unique and stylish setting.

A wide variety of exciting materials is used, as well as more conventional paints, tiles and fabrics. There are many superb ideas – both for large and small projects. Fine details can be easily reproduced or used as an inspiration to develop your own ideas in line with your colour schemes and the atmosphere you want to create in your personal living space.

Those with artistic talents might like to try painting freehand panels or sponging, and for those who cannot sew a stitch, there are simple ideas that are both practical and stylish. Most of the projects can be adapted to suit your own living space and will create a fresh and unique ambience.

Choosing a Scheme

Above: This room is inspired by pargeting, a traditional technique in which wet plaster is imprinted with simple patterns.

BEFORE PLUNGING STRAIGHT for the colour cards and paint pots, take time to think exactly what you want to achieve when you decorate your home. You need to consider whether the scheme you are choosing will succeed in the room you wish to paint.

Take a good look at the room. Which direction does it face and how much light does it receive? There is a world of difference between a room that receives almost no direct sunlight and one that will be sunny and bright for much of the day. If east-or west-facing it may receive sunlight only in the morning or afternoon. Light can radically change the appearance of colours. The shape of the room can also have some bearing, as light may be angled more strongly in some areas depending on the position of the windows, doors and alcoves.

Right: Create a traditional and comfortable room by using dragging (strié) to imitate warm wood panelling.

Left: Giant Japanese motifs are a simple and eye-catching decorative device for bringing forward a wide expanse of wall.

Look at the colours that are already in the room. There may be much that you cannot change, such as furniture, carpets and curtains, and you will have to plan your colours and effects around these. Figure out your scheme with these fixed items in mind.

Choose colours and effects for the atmosphere that you want to create – warm and cosy or cool and spacious. They can also be used to give the visual impression of changing the shape of a room. Warm colours seem to advance, so use these if you want to make a room look smaller. Cool colours recede and are useful for making a room look bigger. Similarly, dark tones tend to advance and light tones recede, so use shades of colour to move space visually. For instance, if you have a high ceiling that you wish to appear lower, paint it in a dark colour. You can also emphasize certain elements in the room in this way, bringing forward awkwardly shaped areas or pushing them back with light tones.

Below: Bold, clean stripes give a modern contemporary feel to this city apartment. Wide stripes have an even greater impact if they are painted over skirting boards (baseboards).

$\mathscr{P}$ATTERNS

Above: The band of tartan colour at dado (chair) rail height helps to lift an otherwise sombre room, as well as retaining its air of formality, suitable for a study or library, such as this.

PATTERN CAN BE USED TO CHANGE SPACE, TOO. Large motifs tend to attract the eye, so use them in areas that you wish to bring forward. Small patterns tend to merge into an overall textured effect unless you are close to them. Vertical patterns such as stripes will give the impression of heightening an area, while horizontal ones will widen it. Remember that texture will also have some effect by breaking up the surface, either reflecting the light or casting small shadows, creating a look that may be similar to a patterned one.

Bear in mind the age of the building you are decorating. Consider whether a particular style or theme is appropriate to the architecture. There may be existing original features that you can plan a theme around. Perhaps you can adapt elements in the design of the furniture

Right: Using a Gustavian-influenced wall stamp is an effective method of making patterns on walls.

Left: A simple and quick way of creating even stripes is to use textured brown paper as a wall treatment.

or fittings to create a completely original theme. A motif from the design of the curtains, for instance, can be used as a basis for a stencil or stamp pattern. Perhaps the style of the fabric would be enhanced with faux effects such as verdigris candlesticks, pewter vases or copper plates. Let your imagination run wild.

Try out your ideas on paper. Even a rough sketch with the colours and the main elements of the room in place will help you see whether the scheme will work and alert you to what you might need to change. Use paint samples so that you are accurate in your choice of colour. The more care you take in planning, the more successful the result is likely to be. Above all, plan a room that you will enjoy decorating and using.

The amount of time and money you have available for decorating are important considerations. If you have only limited time, choose an effect that you will be able to complete.

Below: There is a huge selection of textured, coloured paper available to create interesting wall patterns.

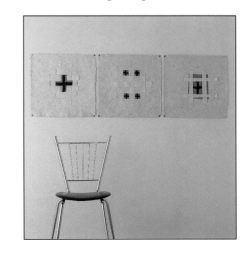

*C*HOOSING FABRICS

Above: The quality of fake furs is now very high and they make great soft cushions, throws and floor coverings.

Furnishing fabrics are more durable than dressmaking materials and, in particular, the colours are less likely to fade, which can be an important consideration when you are making curtains, for example. There are, however, many less expensive alternatives which can make a striking and stylish statement when used outside their normal context. Canvas, for example, is heavy-duty and available in both deep and pastel shades. In addition, it can be stapled and hemmed with double-sided carpet tape, making it very easy to use. Cotton and linen sheets, easily adapted for draped curtains, have a beautifully crisp texture and may be plain or patterned in a vast array of colours.

Right: Simple, elegant curtains can be made out of thick cotton sheets which already have sewn edges.

Left: A modern fabric stretched taut on a wall can create a dramatic wall-hanging and hide any uneven wall surfaces underneath.

It is worth keeping an eye open in second-hand clothes stores and at flea markets for trimmings to add to cushions, curtains and throws. A pretty piece of old lace or a single unusual motif makes a delightful panel inset on a plain cushion cover, for example, or curtains can be trimmed with a contrasting border of old brocade.

Inexpensive plain fabrics can be enhanced with details to give them a unique and much more interesting quality with minimum effort and expense. Rope, for example, is wonderfully versatile because it is so flexible and easy to use. It can be coiled, plaited (braided), twisted or swirled to make a textural border to a valance, curtains, cushion or sofa. Use it singly or in pairs, for self-coloured or contrasting decoration. Similarly, fringes and buttons are inexpensive ways to add colour and eye-catching detail.

Below: Blankets come in bright jewel-like colours and make thick curtains that are excellent draught excluders.

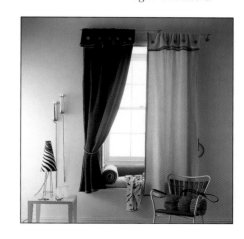

JAPANESE LIVING ROOM

A TECHNIQUE CALLED ROLLER FIDGETING is used to create the warm-looking walls of this traditional Japanese-style living room. Two paint colours mix and merge on the wall as they are applied, providing an ideal ground for a simple freehand leaf design. A painted bamboo panel worked in richer artist's oil colours adds an air of authenticity and is fun to paint. Finally, the furniture is given a smooth lacquered finish to complement the setting.

YOU WILL NEED

emulsion (latex) paint in off-white, sand yellow, pale cream and blue or plum

wide household paintbrushes

roller tray

masonry paint roller

pencil

fine artist's brush

satin or gloss finish paint in pale yellow

artist's oil paint in yellow ochre and burnt umber

white spirit (turpentine)

small paint kettle (pot)

tape measure

fine lining brush

coffee table

fine grade sandpaper

gloss finish paint in blue or plum

spray gloss enamel in blue or plum

spray gloss varnish

one *Apply a coat of off-white emulsion (latex) paint to the wall and leave it to dry thoroughly.*

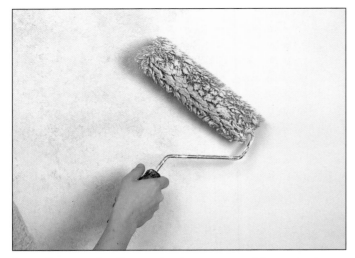

two *Pour sand yellow and pale cream emulsion paint into each side of a roller tray. Coat a masonry roller with the paint and apply it to the wall in random directions, making sure that you do not totally cover the base coat.*

three *When the wall is dry, mark the position of the leaf spray border design with a pencil. Draw the centre lines, making sure they are equally spaced around the room, then draw in the leaves freehand.*

four *Use an artist's brush to paint in the main stalk in plum emulsion (latex). Then paint in the leaves in plum. Some parts of the design may need a second coat.*

five *Apply two coats of pale yellow satin or gloss finish paint to the panels and leave to dry thoroughly. Mix yellow ochre artist's oil paint with white spirit (turpentine) into a creamy consistency in a paint kettle (pot). Drag (strié) the mixture over the surface and leave to dry thoroughly.*

six *Draw pencil lines 1cm (½in) apart in the direction of the dragging (strié), then draw in the slightly round ends of the bamboo. Make sure that there are not too many or the effect will be too complicated.*

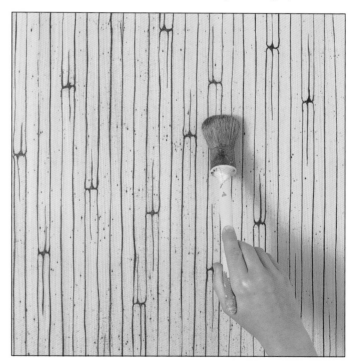

seven *Mix burnt umber artist's paint with white spirit (turpentine) in a paint kettle (pot) to a thick cream. With a fine lining brush, draw over the pencil lines, adding elongated lines from the middle of the bamboo ends about 12.5cm (5in) long. Flick tiny dots of the paint over the surface and soften with the edge of a brush, moving downwards.*

➤

eight *Sand the surface of the table until it is smooth. Clean to ensure that it is free of dust. Apply a base coat of blue or plum gloss paint and leave to dry thoroughly. Sand the surface again to ensure total smoothness. Apply a second base coat and leave to dry thoroughly.*

nine *Spray on blue or plum gloss enamel and leave to dry thoroughly. Spray a gloss varnish over the surface to protect and finish it.*

Fabric Wall

No special sewing skills are needed to achieve this dramatic wall treatment. Draping fabric on a wall is a good way to disguise lumps and bumps and add a lot of interest for little effort. When you have a modern fabric design, however, such as this eye-catching blanket, it may not seem appropriate to drape it on the wall in baroque folds. Instead, create a contemporary look by pulling it as taut as possible with coloured string at the corners and middle of the fabric.

YOU WILL NEED

tape measure
fabric or blanket
pencil
drill, with masonry bit
wall plugs (plastic anchors)
screw eyelets
coloured string
matching strong cotton
thread

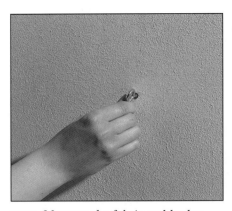

one *Measure the fabric or blanket and mark the positions for the screw eyelets on the wall, bearing in mind that you want the fabric to be pulled very taut. Drill and insert wall plugs (plastic anchors) at the pencil marks. Screw the eyelets securely into the wall.*

two *Wrap lengths of string tightly around the corners of the fabric and also around a small pinch of fabric in the middle of the two long edges.*

three *Feed the strings through the eyelets, pull them tight and secure them by looping the string back on itself and binding it with cotton, for a neat finish.*

MANHATTAN ROOM

THIS MINIMALIST, YET STRIKING, striped wall provides an interesting backdrop to a room that is a haven away from the hubbub of city life. The impact of these wide stripes is maximized by taking them right over the skirting board (baseboard) to floor level. A plain beech effect is used to paint the table top, and the surface pattern and texture is achieved by using a heart grainer (rocker) and comb. The techniques are easy to master. Finally, remember to varnish the table to protect your handiwork.

YOU WILL NEED

emulsion (latex) paint in off-white and coffee
household paintbrushes
long ruler
spirit (carpenter's) level
pencil
wide paint pad
table
satin finish paint in white
artist's oil colour paint in yellow ochre
white spirit (turpentine)
paint kettle (pot)
heart grainer (rocker)
graduated comb
narrow comb
varnish and brush

one *Apply two coats of off-white emulsion (latex) paint to the wall and leave to dry completely.*

two *Using a long ruler and a spirit (carpenter's) level, measure 30cm (12in) wide stripes, marking them out with a pencil.*

three *Paint the alternate bands using a wide paint pad and coffee paint. Concentrate on the edges before filling in the inside of the bands.*

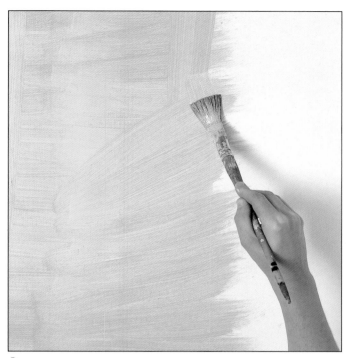

four *To paint the beech effect table, apply two coats of white satin finish paint as a base coat. Leave each one to dry completely. Mix yellow ochre artist's oil paint with white spirit (turpentine) to the consistency of thick cream, then brush it evenly over the surface.*

five *Drag (strié) the surface of the paint in a single lengthways direction.*

six *Use a heart grainer (rocker) to start making the graining. Do this by pulling the tool down gently, slightly rocking it and working in several spaced lines. Do not butt the lines up together.*

➤

seven *With a graduated comb, work in the same direction and fill in the lines between the heart graining.*

eight *Again, working in the same direction, soften the effect with a large, dry brush.*

nine *Using a narrow comb, go over the entire surface in the same direction to add detail to the effect. Varnish when dry.*

PARCHMENT PAPER ART

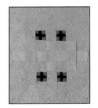

THERE IS SUCH AN INTERESTING VARIETY of textured and coloured papers available from ordinary stationery stores as well as specialist art and craft suppliers that it is easy to find the right basic ingredients to make some simple but extremely effective pictures, without being skilled at painting. Choose your colour combination and then make slits in the background paper, through which to weave the contrasting colours. These contrasting papers don't need to be clean-cut; in fact, tearing their edges actually enhances the finished look.

YOU WILL NEED

parchment paper sheets
coloured paper sheets
scrap paper
pencil
metal ruler
craft knife
self-healing cutting mat

one *Decide on the most interesting combination of papers. Use ordinary scrap paper to plan your design first before cutting the parchment.*

two *Draw lines on the scrap paper where you want the slits to be.*

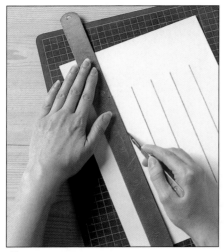

three *Laying the paper on the cutting mat, cut these slits carefully with the craft knife.*

four *Weave paper through the slits. When you are happy with the design, rework using parchment.*

COLONIAL PANELLING

ONE OF THE EASIEST METHODS FOR CREATING a wood panel effect is to use the technique of dragging (strié). Simply pull the wet paint with the tips of the bristles of a dry brush in the direction of the wood grain. The technique creates a maximum impact in rooms where large areas of panelling are required, such as this colonial-style living room. It is important to keep the lines in each vertical or horizontal section clean and unbroken, so make sure you plan panels that can be covered with a comfortable stroke of the brush.

YOU WILL NEED

emulsion (latex) paint in off-white and mid-brown (medium brown)
household paintbrushes
long ruler
pencil
masking tape
wallpaper paste
paint kettle (pot)

one *Apply two coats of off-white paint as a base coat for the panelling. Leave to dry. Then, using a long ruler and pencil, measure and mark the height and size of the panelling you require.*

two *Mask off the dado (chair) rail. Mix the brown paint with 50 per cent wallpaper paste in a paint kettle (pot). Brush the paint mixture over the dado (chair) rail area. Using a dry brush, drag (strié) along the middle of the rail in a horizontal direction to remove some of the paint and create a highlight effect. Apply masking tape to the borders of the main panels, mitring the corners, and similarly paint and then drag (strié) the panels in a vertical direction.*

three *Mask off the top and bottom sections and paint and then drag them in a horizontal direction.*

four *Remove the tape, except from the centre panel border. Brush the brown paint mixture on to the side panels and drag down in a vertical direction. Leave the paint to dry thoroughly.*

five *Remove the tape from the right-hand side and bottom of the centre panels and paint in two coats of the brown mixture to give a darker shadow effect.*

➤

six *Remove the tape from the top of the centre panels and paint in a coat of the brown mixture and drag (strié) the inner edge to create a highlight. Repeat the process for the left-hand side.*

Above: Mitred edges enable you to paint in realistic highlights and shadows to give the illusion of depth to the painted panels. You can achieve the effect easily by mitring the masking tape first before applying it and then removing it length by length as you paint each edge.

SANTA FE WALLS

AZTEC MOTIFS, SUCH AS THIS BIRD, are bold, stylized and two-dimensional, and translate perfectly into stamps. Strong colour contrasts suit this style, but here the pattern is confined to widely spaced strips over a cool white wall, and further restrained with a final light wash of white paint over the stamped motifs.

YOU WILL NEED

matt (flat) emulsion (latex) paint in off-white, warm white, deep red and navy blue

paint kettle (pot)

natural sponge

broad and medium household paintbrushes

plumb line

ruler

pencil

masking tape

felt-tipped pen

medium-density sponge, such as a household sponge

craft knife

self-healing cutting mat

small paint roller

old plate

high-density sponge, such as upholstery foam (foam rubber)

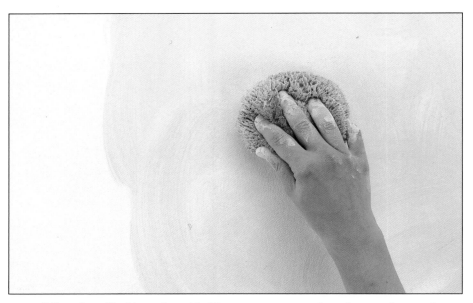

one *Dilute the off-white paint with 50 per cent water and apply a wash over the wall using a natural sponge, alternating the angle at which you work. Allow to dry.*

two *Using a broad, dry brush, apply warm white paint to some areas of the wall to achieve a rough-looking surface. Allow to dry.*

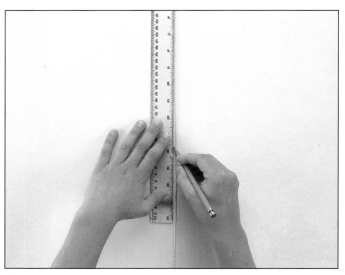

three *Starting 10cm (4in) from one corner, and using a plumb line as a guide, draw a straight line from the top to the bottom of the wall.*

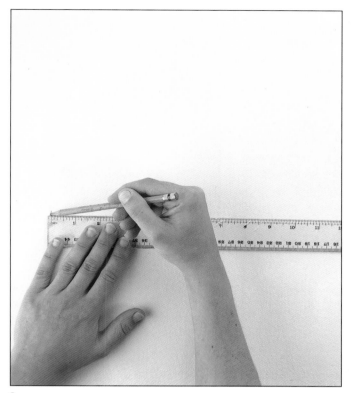

four *Measure 45cm (17¾in) along the wall, hang the plumb line again and mark a second vertical line. Draw another line 10cm (4in) away to create a band. Repeat all across the wall.*

five *Apply masking tape to the wall on each outer edge of the marked bands. Paint the bands in deep red emulsion (latex). Leave to dry.*

six *Draw a 10 x 20cm (4 x 8in) diamond shape on a medium-density sponge and cut out the shape using a craft knife and cutting mat.*

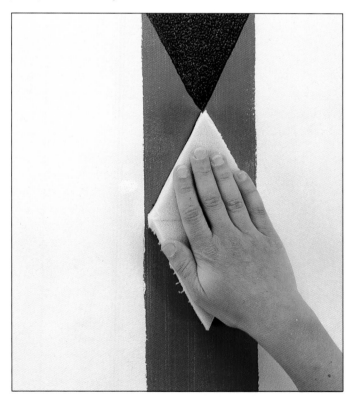

seven *Use a small roller to load the stamp with navy blue paint and stamp the diamonds down the red bands, starting from the top and just touching at their tips.*

➤

four *Draw two intersecting lines across the back of the composition (mat) board and glue a wooden drawer knob in the centre to finish the stamp.*

five *Attach a plumb line at ceiling height to give a vertical guideline (this can be done with a piece of masking tape) on the wall. Mark a point 8cm (3¼in) above the dado (chair) rail and place one corner of the cardboard square on it, lined up along the plumb line. Mark all the corners of the cardboard square on the wall in pencil, then move it up, continuing to mark the corners. Use this system to mark a grid of squares across the whole surface of the upper wall.*

six *One of the stamps has a static motif and the other has a swirl. Use the static one first, dipping it into a plate coated with paint and making the first print on a sheet of scrap paper to make sure that the stamp is not overloaded. Then print diagonally up the wall from the 8cm (3¼in) mark. Continue printing, working diagonally up the wall.*

seven *Change to the swirl motif and stamp this pattern in the spaces between the static motifs.*

➤

eight *Use a pencil and ruler to draw a line 4cm (1½in) above the level of the dado (chair) rail, all the way along the stamped section of wall.*

nine *Fill the space between the pencil line and the dado (chair) rail with dark blue paint, using a square-tipped paintbrush.*

ℰТHNIC PATTERNS

THIS ROOM IS INSPIRED by pargeting, a traditional technique in which wet plaster is imprinted with simple patterns. This painted version, with mock panels on either side, would make a feature of an awkward window. Experiment with thinning the paint – it should flow smoothly off the brush. Instead of a painter's mahl stick (maul stick), you can tape a small wad of cotton wool (absorbent cotton) covered with lint or chamois leather to the end of a stick.

YOU WILL NEED

emulsion (latex) paint in white

artist's acrylic paints: yellow ochre and burnt umber

large household paintbrush

ruler

pencil

straight edge

pair of compasses (compass)

mahl stick (maul stick)

artist's watercolour brush

one *Tint some white emulsion (latex) with yellow ochre to make a soft straw yellow. Dilute with water to make a thin, milky glaze. Brush on to the wall, varying the direction of your strokes to give an uneven colour.*

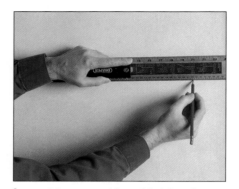

two *Measure a 10cm (4in) border around the window, using a straight edge, and draw lightly in pencil. Leave a gap of 15cm (6in), then draw a panel on either side of the window. The width of the panel should be half the window width. Draw a 10cm (4in) border inside each panel.*

three *Using a pair of compasses (compass), draw two circles inside each panel. Draw quarter circles in the corners.*

four *Practise holding the mahl stick (maul stick) against the wall with your spare hand to support your painting hand. Mix some burnt umber into the paint and paint over the border outlines.*

five *Add the diamond shapes freehand, painting stripes first in one direction and then the other.*

six *Allow the brush to create the corner motifs. Touch the point of the brush down, then splay it out as you curve into the corner.*

seven *Add smooth curves within each circle to represent the stylized wheel spokes.*

eight *Fill in the vertical panels with diagonal stripes.*

PARQUET EFFECT

GOOD PARQUET IS A very manageable kind of flooring. There are numerous patterns to be made from combining these wooden blocks. A good trick is to work out the pattern starting from the centre and make it as big a perfect square as you can; then lay a simple border to accommodate all the tricky outside edges. Parquet is often in oak but you could dye it with stain or varnish for a richer effect.

YOU WILL NEED

pencil and string

ridged adhesive spreader

PVA (white) glue floor adhesive

parquet blocks

timber length

matt (flat) varnish

varnish brush

fine-grade sandpaper

one *Make sure your floor surface is clean, dry and level. Find your starting point by stretching string from corner to corner as for tiles and draw guidelines on the floor. Using a ridged spreader, coat a small area of floor with adhesive.*

two *Apply parquet blocks to the adhesive. Use a length of timber laid across the blocks to check that they all lie flush. Repeat until the floor is covered. Seal the floor with two or three coats of varnish, sanding between coats.*

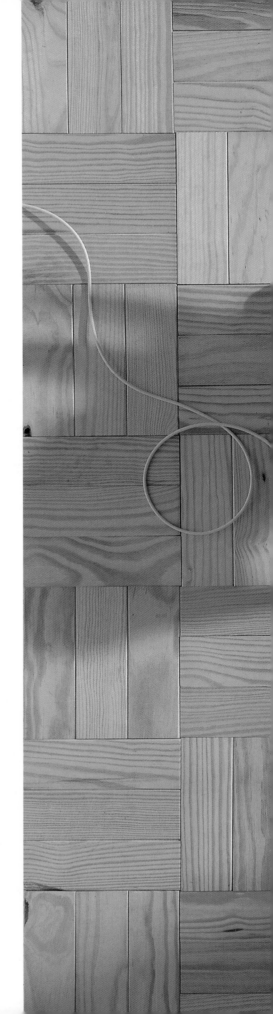

FLOATING FLOOR

WOOD-STRIP FLOORING IS a good way of creating instant elegance. It comes in a huge variety of finishes and lengths, so you can combine different woods without difficulty. Once you have mastered the principles of how to lay it, you can work out many different combinations and patterns. The main photograph shows walnut interspersed with wide, light-coloured maple boards. Alternatively, choose just one wood and lay it in different patterns. Laminated types of wood strip are generally pre-finished but others need to be sealed once they have been laid.

YOU WILL NEED

cushioned underlay (optional)

sticky tape

metal joint clips

hammer

wood-strip flooring

spacers and lever

wood glue

packing

saw

tacks and quadrant beading (optional)

pencil (optional)

drill, with wood bit (optional)

one *If you are using underlay, unroll it and tape one end to keep it in place. Prepare all the boards of wood strip by hammering the special metal joint clips into the groove on the underside of the board, along the tongued edge.*

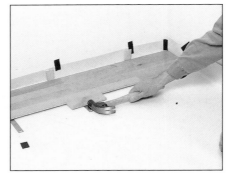

two *Lay the first length, clips towards you, against the walls, using spacers. Glue the ends of butt-jointed lengths. Position the second row, tapping them together with a hammer and an offcut (scrap), so that the clips engage in the groove of the second row.*

three *Cut the last board to width, allowing for spacers, and apply glue along its grooved edge. Insert packing against the wall before levering the strip into place. Tamp it level with a hammer, using an offcut for protection.*

four *Replace the skirting board (baseboard) or tack lengths of quadrant beading to hide the expansion gap; make sure the skirting board fits tightly against the floor.*

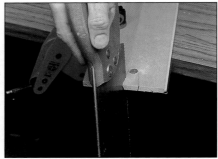

five *To fit a board around a pipe, mark its position and drill a suitably sized hole. Then cut out a tapered wedge, which can be glued back after fitting the board.*

SHEET-METAL TREAD MATS

SHEET-METAL TREAD MATS are a versatile and hard-wearing floor covering and will give a room a unique look. They may be painted – either plain or patterned – but also look absolutely dazzling left in their natural state. The sheets come in a wide range of metals, including copper, zinc and stainless steel, and can be cut to size by the shop. Lay the sheets on concrete or a subfloor of hardboard, chipboard or marine-plywood.

YOU WILL NEED

sheet metal tread mats

metal file

floor adhesive (optional)

wood scrap (optional)

drill, with metal pilot drill bit, and wood drill bit (optional)

wood screws (optional)

screwdriver (optional)

metal or wooden quadrant beading

one *File away any rough edges with a metal file, but be careful not to create file marks on the top surface of the sheets. If you have a concrete floor, the metal sheets can be glued directly in place. If you are laying sheets on wood, use a piece of wood as a rest and a metal pilot drill bit to drill holes in every corner of the mats and at intervals of 20cm (8in) along all the sides, depending on the size of the sheets.*

two *If you are laying the metal sheets over wooden floorboards, you can screw through the holes in the metal directly into the wood surface with wood screws.*

three *Butt up the sheets together and continue screwing them to the floor. To finish, fit metal or wooden quadrant beading around the edges.*

RUBBER MATS

AVAILABLE FROM RUBBER MANUFACTURERS, this safety matting is valued for its non-slip and protective qualities, and since it is waterproof, it is particularly useful in, say, a shower room. Rubber matting doesn't fray when cut and will happily absorb any lumps or strange joins in a floor. Clean and seal the matting with a silicone spray polish, then fix it in place using any rubber contact adhesive. Make sure your floor is sanded, or lay an MDF (medium-density fiberboard) layer underneath before starting.

YOU WILL NEED

2 types of rubber safety mat
tape measure
metal rule or straight edge
craft knife
Pirelli rubber tiles in
different patterns
rubber contact adhesive
WD-40 or silicone spray

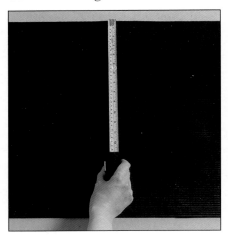

one *Measure the floor and the rubber matting and carefully trim the matting to size.*

two *For the corners, cut four squares. Divide these diagonally and make four squares by placing two triangles together, with the grooves running across and top to bottom. Position these and the runners around the edge of the room.*

three *Cut pieces from the other matting to fit the central section. Cut the tiles into squares, then cut holes in the mat at regular intervals to take the squares.*

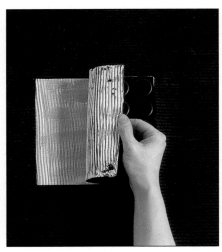

four *Secure all the pieces with rubber adhesive, applied to both surfaces. Spray with WD-40 or silicone spray.*

TEXTURED FLOOR MATS

FLOOR MATS ARE EASILY available, extremely cheap and particularly useful as you can usually cut them without their edges fraying. They are manufactured in many finishes, some even incorporating words, symbols or pictures, and all are produced in manageable rectangles. When these heavily textured grey polypropylene mats are arranged with the pile alternately running in different directions, a delightful checkerboard effect is achieved. For a different style of room, you could create a less subtle or even thoroughly funky effect by combining two or more colours. Make sure your floor surface is smooth before starting.

YOU WILL NEED

string

white crayon or chalk

tape measure

grey polypropylene floor mats

long metal ruler or straight edge

craft knife

notched spreader

floor adhesive

one *Use strings stretched across to find the room's centre and mark with a cross. Link the opposite pairs of walls. Measure the floor and work out how many floor mats you will need. Mark the cuts with a white crayon or chalk on the reverse of the floor mats.*

two *If the mats are of carpet quality, first score along the lines before cutting them with the craft knife. Then cut the mats to size.*

three *Using a notched spreader, apply floor adhesive to the floor.*

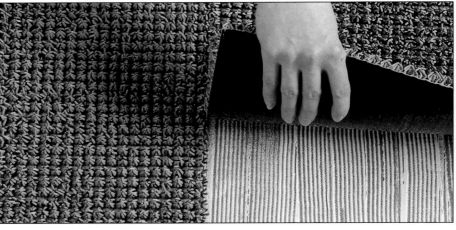

four *Starting at the centre, carefully lay the mats in position, remembering that, for the checkerboard effect shown here, you need to alternate the weaves.*

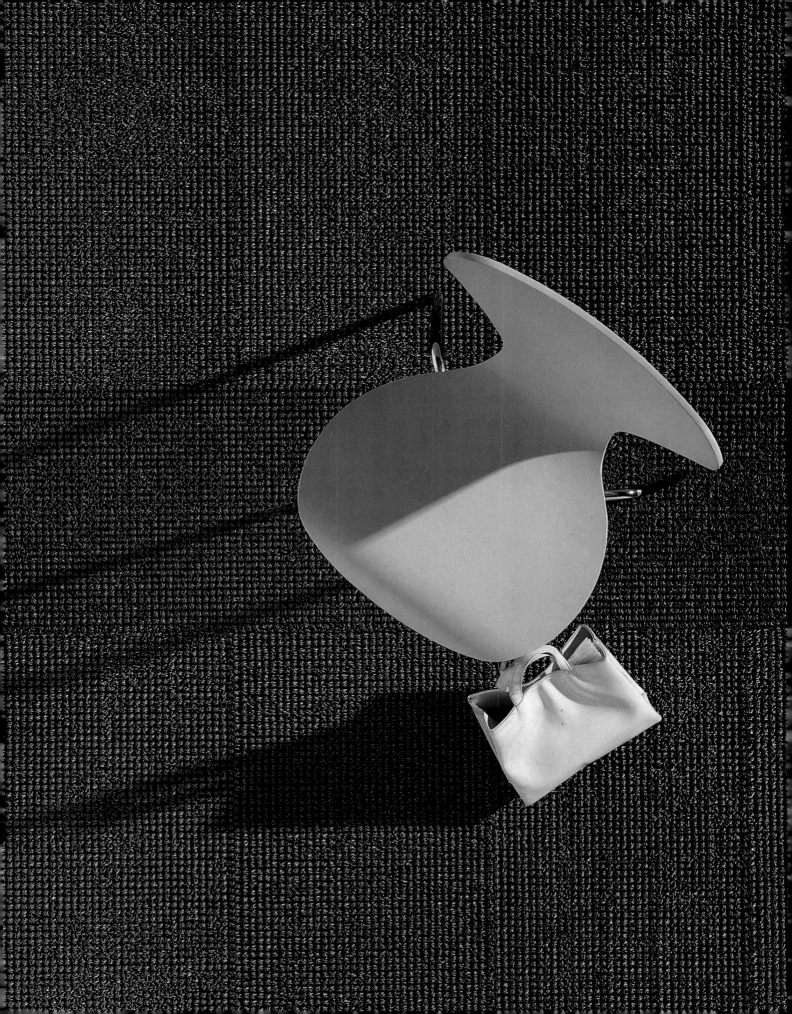

CHECKERBOARD FLOOR

CORK IS A WONDERFUL NATURAL MATERIAL that provides a warm, quiet and relatively cheap floor covering. It has been largely confined to the kitchen and bathroom in the past, but should not be overlooked when choosing a floor for living areas. It is important to lay the tiles on an even surface, so tack a layer of hardboard across the floorboards first.

YOU WILL NEED

cork floor tiles

woodstains in dark Jacobean Oak and Antique Pine

large household paintbrush

tape measure

straight edge and craft knife

cork-tile adhesive and spreader (optional)

clear satin finish varnish and brush

one *Paint half the tiles with dark Jacobean Oak woodstain and the remaining tiles with the Antique Pine woodstain and leave to dry overnight. Measure the floor length to establish the number of dark tiles needed and cut half that number in half diagonally. Begin laying the dark half tiles in the corner that will be seen most, and work along one wall. If using self-adhesive tiles, simply peel off the backing.*

two *Lay the contrasting tiles next, tight up against the first row, wiping off any excess adhesive that has been forced up between the tiles, if you are using adhesive. Once you have laid the two rows, measure the nearest adjoining wall and cut half tiles to fit that length as well. Stick these down.*

three *Now, work to fill the floor space diagonally. Trim the tiles at the opposite edges of the room to fit snugly against the skirting board (baseboard). Apply two coats of clear varnish to seal the floor. It is important to make sure that the first coat is thoroughly dry before you apply the next.*

DREAMY COTTON DRAPES

A PAIR OF COTTON SHEETS makes the most wonderful drape and all the seams are perfectly finished. The bigger the sheets, the more luxurious and elegant the window will look – drapes should always be generous. Wooden pegs can be wedged into a piece of old wooden floorboarding or driftwood – if you drill the holes at an angle, the fixing will be stronger as well as more decorative.

YOU WILL NEED

scissors

cotton tape, 2.5 m
(2½ yds)

2 flat king-size cotton sheets

needle and white sewing
thread

drill with masonry and wood
drill bits

length of floorboarding or
driftwood, window width
plus 15cm (6in) either side

6 old-fashioned wooden pegs

spirit (carpenter's) level

wall plugs (plastic anchors)
and screws

screwdriver

one *With scissors, cut the cotton tape into six strips of equal length.*

two *Divide the width of each sheet top by three and use the divisions as points to attach the tapes. Fold each tape in half and use small stitches to sew them to the top of the sheet.*

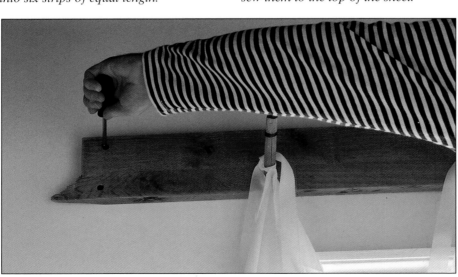

three *Drill six holes at equal distances along the floorboarding and wedge in the pegs. Drill a hole either end of the floorboarding. Screw the boarding into the wall, using a spirit (carpenter's) level, and appropriate fixings to secure it.*

four *Tie the tapes securely and neatly to the pegs and arrange the drapes.*

CREAM TOPPING

MAKE A GRAND STATEMENT at the window by creating a pelmet with a curved edge trimmed with rope. The gentle wave of the pelmet gives a very gracious, elegant appearance to the treatment, which could, if you wish, be echoed in the edging of a loose cover on a chair or sofa. Another wonderful idea is to continue the pelmet right around the top of the room, so it acts as a wavy trim to the whole area. In this instance make sure the pelmet is the same colour as the ceiling so it doesn't interrupt the eye's progress. Pelmets can be any shape or size; experiment with pointed Vs with bells on, castellations and the like. Cut the shape out of paper first, and pin it above the curtains to see what effect it will have upon the window and the room as a whole.

YOU WILL NEED

tape measure

2 plates

paper, for pattern

pencil

pelmet fabric

dressmaker's scissors

interfacing

dressmaker's pins

needle and tacking (basting) thread

sewing machine

matching sewing thread

iron

rope

wooden batten

drill and bits

wall plugs

screws and screwdriver

hammer and tacks or Velcro

one *Measure the window and decide on the dimensions of the pelmet. Allow an extra 5cm (2in) to attach to the batten. Use plates to make a pattern.*

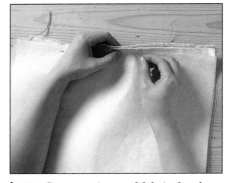

two *Cut two pieces of fabric for the back and the front of the pelmet. Cut out interfacing to stiffen the pelmet, and pin the three layers together with right sides facing.*

three *Draw round the pattern on to the pelmet piece with a pencil. Pin the fabric just inside the outline.*

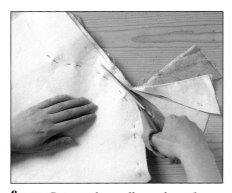

four *Cut out the scallops about 1cm (½in) from the outline. Tack (baste) along the edge, then machine-stitch.*

five *Trim the interfacing and clip the seam allowance so that the curves will lie flat when turned right-side out.*

six *Turn the pelmet right-side out and press the scalloped edge. Turn under the straight edge of the pelmet, then pin and machine-stitch.*

seven *Measure the scalloped edge, and cut a length of rope to fit. Experiment with design options for the rope; for example, you could use two different colours and weights of rope.*

eight *Pin the rope to the pelmet and hand-sew it in place. To attach the pelmet to the wall, use a slim batten of wood and nail the pelmet to it; alternatively, use Velcro to make the pelmet easy to remove.*

DRAWING-ROOM SECRETS

JUST BECAUSE YOU INVEST heavily in some great curtain fabric, you should not feel committed to spending at least as much again on having it made up. This is a totally no-sew curtain and pelmet idea that could easily pass for the work of a professional! To work out how much material you need, just measure the drop and allow three times that length. The seams are all iron-on and the rest is done with a staple gun and string. It's hard to imagine that such an elegant draped pelmet could be put together without sewing a stitch. Follow the steps to discover the hidden secrets that lie behind this drawing-room window.

YOU WILL NEED

striped fabric

scissors

iron-on hem fix (such as Wundaweb) or double-sided carpet tape (optional)

iron

2 wooden battens, window width, plus 30cm (12in) each side

spirit (carpenter's) level

drill and drill bits

wall plugs (plastic anchors) and screws

screwdriver

staple gun

string

one *Divide the fabric into three equal lengths, two for the curtains and one for the pelmet. Turn over the hems on both ends of the pelmet and one end of each of the curtains. Attach the hems with iron-on hem fix, or carpet tape if the fabric is heavy. Attach the thin side of one of the battens to the wall so that the ends overlap the window equally – use a spirit (carpenter's) level to check the position. Screw the other length of wood on to it at a right angle.* ➤

two *Starting at one end, staple the edge of one curtain to the front of the batten, inserting the staples vertically. Staple the other corner of the curtain to the middle of the batten. Most of the curtain fabric will now hang loose in the middle.*

three *For the pleats, hold the curtain away from the window and find the middle. Staple this to the middle of the batten. Find the middle of the two loose sections. Staple them to the middle of the batten. Keep sub-dividing batten and fabric until you reach the pleat width you want. Repeat for the other curtain so that it matches.*

four *Fold the pelmet fabric in half lengthways and line up with the centre of the window. Starting at the centre, staple along one edge to the top of the batten, close to the wall. Lift the side drops and gather up the fabric at the corners. Put a row of staples under the gather so that the stripes line up with the curtain stripes below.*

five *Bunch up the fabric at each corner and tie it with string. Be aware of the way the fabric folds at this stage – you may need to practise folding and tying a few times until you achieve the desired effect. Staple the string to the batten. It won't show, so use as many staples as you like to make it secure.*

six *Tie another piece of string around the drop of the pelmet, about 30cm (12in) down. Tie it tightly, leaving enough string to allow you to tie another knot to attach this section to the top corner.*

seven *Pull the fabric up to the corner and tie the string ends around the first knot. Push the knots inside the remaining fabric to puff the front out. If necessary, add staples to hold this in place along the top of the batten. Finally, arrange the pleats and folds.*

No-Frills Navy

BLOCK OUT THE LIGHT with these crisp, stylish navy blue curtains. Cotton duck (canvas) is as heavy as denim, but to add firmness and thickness to the tops, you can use double-sided carpet tape to bond them together. This also means that you get a good fit with the large brass eyelets that are made for tent canvas and sails. You will need to buy fabric about one and a half times the width of your window, plus an allowance of 5cm (2in) at the top and bottom to get perfect pleats. It is always a good idea to be generous with curtain material, so stretch the budget rather than the fabric.

YOU WILL NEED

double-sided carpet tape
craft knife
navy cotton duck (canvas)
backing card (cardboard)
ruler
pencil
hole punch
hammer
brass eyelets
rigging wire, window width
2 wire rope grips
2 thimbles
pliers (optional)
drill and bits
2 wall plugs (plastic anchors) and large hooks

one *Stick a length of double-sided carpet tape along the top of the fabric, just in from the edge. Peel off the top paper. Fold the top hem over the tape, smoothing as you go to ensure a crisp, wrinkle-free finish.*

two *Place the curtain on a sheet of backing card (cardboard). Using a ruler and a pencil, mark the positions for the holes at 20cm (8in) intervals. Put the back part of the hole punch in position behind the fabric to make the first hole.*

three *Position the top part of the hole punch and bang it firmly with a hammer. Place the back part of the eyelet in the back part of the hole punch. Fit the middle of the eyelet through the punched hole.*

four *Place the top half of the eyelet on top of the bottom half. Position the tool provided with the eyelets and bang it firmly with a hammer. Continue positioning the eyelets at the marked intervals along the top of the curtains.*

five *Thread the rigging wire through the wire grip to form a loop. Place the thimble inside the loop and pull the wire taut. Using a hammer on a hard surface, bang the wire grip closed. You may also need to squeeze it with pliers.*

six *Drill holes and fix one of the hooks in the window recess. Loop the rigging wire over it. Thread the curtains on to the rigging wire through the eyelets.*

seven *Thread the other end through the wire grip as before, then attach to a hook. Screw the hook into a pre-drilled and plugged hole. This will ensure even pleats.*

No-PROBLEM LINKS

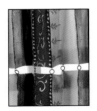

WHAT LENGTHS WILL YOU GO TO for a bargain? If you find the fabric of your dreams in the remnant bin, but it's just that bit too short for your window, it's no longer a problem. Use curtain rings to connect the different lengths of fabric you have found – you can use as many as you need for the drop. Nobody will ever suspect that the linked effect was anything other than a deliberate design decision.

YOU WILL NEED

drill and bits

spirit (carpenter's) level

wall plugs (plastic anchors)
and screws

screwdriver

metal curtain rail and fixings

assorted lengths of remnant
fabrics

iron-on hem fix
(such as Wundaweb,
optional)

iron

needle and matching
sewing thread

split curtain rings

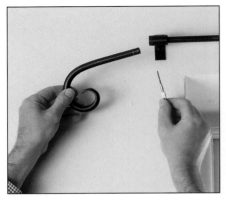

one *Attach the rail fixings above the window. Check with a spirit (carpenter's) level before you screw them to the wall. Assemble the rail and fixings.*

two *Hem all the rough edges of the fabric, either with iron-on hem fix or by hand. Sew small split rings along the top edge of the curtain to link into the rail rings. Sew rings in the same positions along the bottom of the first piece of fabric.*

three *Line the curtain up with the next piece of fabric and mark the positions for attaching the rings. Make sure they line up exactly with the first curtain if you have a geometric or striped pattern. Sew the rings to the second piece of fabric along the whole width, then hang in place.*

Above: The curtains can be linked with single rings, split rings or interconnecting rings as shown here.

JAPANESE SCREEN

THIS SCREEN IS THE PERFECT treatment for a minimalist room scheme. It lets you hide from the outside world, yet you can still benefit from the light filtering through. The screen is made from a simple, wooden garden trellis, painted matt (flat) black, with heavyweight tracing paper stapled behind it. Cut the trellis to fit your window recess, but always do it to the nearest square so it looks balanced. The paper is stapled behind the struts.

YOU WILL NEED
garden trellis
blackboard paint
paintbrush
heavyweight tracing paper
staple gun
craft knife (optional)
emulsion (latex) paint in red
drill, with wood bit
2 eyelets
tape measure
wire coat hanger
wire-cutters
pliers
2 picture rail hooks

one *Paint the trellis black and let dry. Blackboard paint creates a perfect matt (flat) finish, but other matt (flat) or gloss paints can be used. Staple sheets of tracing paper on to the back of the trellis. If necessary, trim the tracing paper with a craft knife so that no overlaps or seams are visible from the front.*

two *For added interest, paint one square red and leave to dry. Drill a very fine hole in the top of the trellis, at the first strut in from each end.*

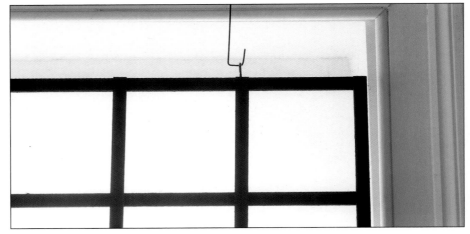

three *Screw an eyelet into each hole. Measure the length of the window to determine how long the hooks for hanging should be. The base of the screen should touch the window frame below. Cut two pieces of coat hanger wire to the correct length for the hooks, then hang the screen on these from picture rail hooks.*

BUTTONED BLANKETS

THESE BLANKETS WERE too brilliant to hide away in the bedroom so they were transformed into an attractive window treatment. They make good draught excluders and are simply rigged up on a couple of towel rails. You need a solid wall as the blankets are weighty. They are doubled over and held together with a row of large safety pins.

one *Attach the towel rails to the wall above the window, by drilling holes and inserting wall plugs (plastic anchors). As towel rails are not long enough, hang them at different heights.*

two *Fold both the blankets in half lengthways. Drape them over the curtain rails, to create a 30cm (12in) pelmet as shown. Take down the blankets. Decide upon the position of the buttons, trying them out by fixing them to the blankets with dressmaker's pins or with double-sided tape.*

three *Stitch the buttons along the pelmet, just catching the first layer with a few stitches to secure the buttons, but without damaging the blanket.*

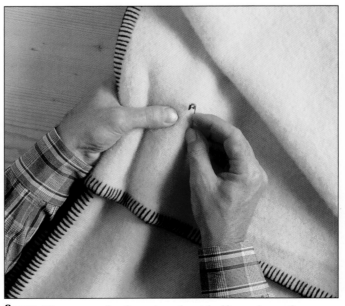

four *Pin a row of safety pins about halfway down the pelmet, on the underside where they won't show. Hang the blankets back in position. Re-pin carefully, so that each safety pin goes through the inside layer of the pelmet, and the outer layer of the curtain.*

MAGIC BEADS

TRANSPARENT BEADS DON'T block out the light or keep out the draughts, but when the sun catches them, they sparkle like jewels, and using them full-length on a square window can turn a light source into something bright and magical. Beads are available in brilliant, gem-like colours, softly co-ordinated pastels and clear colourless textures and each has its own unique, light-enhancing quality.

YOU WILL NEED

2 wooden battens, window width, plus 8–10cm (3–4in) each side

wood glue

hammer

panel pins (brads)

ruler

emulsion (latex) paint in black and white

paintbrush

drill and bits

coloured bead curtain, with fixing strip and screws

screwdriver

wall plugs (plastic anchors) and screws

spirit (carpenter's) level

small jewelled drawer knob

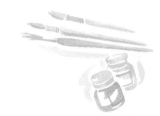

one *Make the pelmet by sticking one edge of a batten to the long edge of the other to form a right angle. Hammer in a few panel pins (brads) to secure it. Divide the length into equal sections and paint them black and white.*

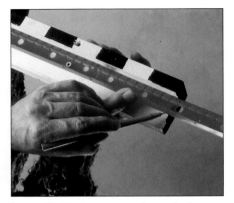

two *Drill, then screw through the holes in the bead fixing strip to secure it underneath the pelmet.*

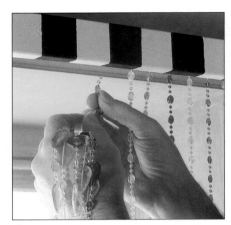

three *Drill, insert wall plugs (plastic anchors) and screw the pelmet in place. Use a spirit (carpenter's) level to check the position after attaching one side. Hang the lengths of beads, in a pattern or at random, along the fixing strip.*

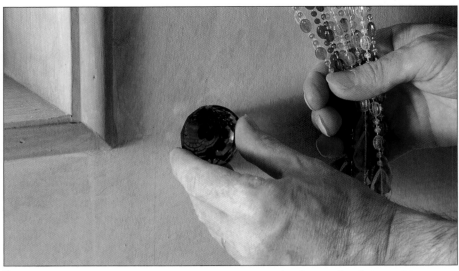

four *Drill a hole, insert a wall plug and screw in the drawer knob in position – level with the base of the window if it is a small one, or halfway down if you have a larger window.*

LIFE'S LITTLE LUXURIES

CUSHIONS ARE THE PERFECT way to add a certain style, as well as an element of comfort, to your room. Here, the choice of natural tones and fabrics perfectly complements the simplicity of the sofa. Interest was added to the restrained look with decorative ties, looped buttons and a simple rope trim. If you want a change from the neutral colour scheme shown here, add splashes of vibrant colour with blues, reds, oranges and purples. Alternatively, blue and white always looks fresh and pretty.

YOU WILL NEED
ROPE-TRIMMED CUSHION
about 2m (2yds) fine-gauge rope
dressmaker's pins
plain linen cushion cover
needle
matching sewing thread
cushion pad

CUSHION WITH TIES
cushion pad
tape measure
cotton duck (canvas)
dressmaker's scissors
dressmaker's pins
needle
tacking (basting) thread
iron
sewing machine
matching sewing thread

LOOP AND BUTTON CUSHION
cushion pad
1m (1yds) linen
tape measure
dressmaker's scissors
dressmaker's pins
needle
tacking (basting) thread
sewing machine
matching sewing thread
small safety pin
iron
8–10 small buttons

one *For the rope-trimmed cushion cover, use a fine-gauge rope to experiment with different designs. When you are happy with the result, pin the rope on to the cover. Hand-stitch the cord to the cover, neatly finishing off the ends. Insert the cushion pad.*

two *For the cushion with ties, measure the cushion pad and cut one piece of cotton duck (canvas) the width of the cushion plus 15mm (⅝in) all around for seams, and a second piece twice the length plus 16cm (6½in) for turning. Pin, baste, press and sew the seams on the wrong side. Turn it right side out.*

three *For the ties, cut six pieces of cotton duck 6 x 28cm (2¼ x 11in). Fold each in half lengthways with wrong sides together and pin, baste, press and machine-stitch a 1cm (½in) seam around two sides. Clip the seams and corners. Turn the ties right-side out and slip-stitch the ends closed. Position the ties in pairs and top-stitch.*

four *For the cushion with loops and buttons, measure the width and length of the cushion pad. Double the length and add 10cm (4in) for the flap opening, plus 3cm (1¼in) for seams all around. You will also need to cut a 7.5cm (3in) wide strip, the width of the cushion plus seams. Cut the linen to this size and fold it in half.*

five *To make the piping for the button loops cut a length of linen about 2.5cm (1in) wide, on the cross. With wrong sides together, pin, baste and machine-stitch the fabric. Trim close to the stitching and, using a small safety pin, turn through to the right side. Press flat.*

six *Measure the buttons and cut the loops to the correct size. Turn over the seam allowance on the cover, then pin and baste the loops in position. Pin, baste and sew the interfacing strip for the back opening on the edge of the cover over the ends of the loops, as shown.*

seven *With the right sides together, sew a seam all around the cushion cover. Turn it right-side out and press. Mark the positions of the buttons with pins, and hand-sew them in place. Insert the cushion pad.*

ANIMAL CUSHIONS

ANIMAL PRINTS HAVE NEVER BEEN more popular and the quality of fake fur now available is truly fantastic. It is also a delight to animal-lovers and the environmentally conscious. The distinctive boldness of the cowhide print chosen here makes great cushion covers. A sofa can be draped with lengths of silky smooth velvet tiger- and leopard-skin fabric that spill over on to the floor, adding to the tactile, languorous atmosphere. This project doesn't have to be a permanent fixture, so bring out these wonderful throws and cushions for wild weekends – or when you want to bring out the animal in you.

YOU WILL NEED
cardboard

scissors

button blanks

small pieces of black velvet

hemmed squares of cowhide print, 5cm (2in) smaller than the cushions

black velvet cushions

needle and thread

tiger- and leopard-skin fabrics

one *Cut a circle of cardboard about 1cm (½in) larger all around than the button blanks. Use the cardboard pattern to cut circles of black velvet.*

two *Cover the top of each button blank with a velvet circle, tucking in the edges so that they catch on to the spikes underneath.*

three *Press the backing firmly in place to make neatly covered black velvet buttons.*

four *Stitch a hemmed cowhide fabric square diagonally on each cushion. Sew a black button on to the centre, stitching through both the cowhide print and the velvet cushion. Drape the fabrics and arrange the cushions on them.*

PAINT CAN LAMP

NECESSITY REALLY IS THE mother of invention. This lamp was designed by a friend stuck in a remote village, who needed a good light to read by. The heavy lamp base is made from a large painted paint can filled with sand, while the shade is a smaller paint can drilled with a pattern of holes. The flex travels inside a curved copper plumbing pipe that is plunged into the sand. The graceful bend of the copper piping can be achieved only by using a special long spring used in the plumbing trade. If you know a friendly plumber, ask for help, otherwise a plumber's merchant should be able to bend the pipe for you. Ask an electrician to wire up the finished lamp for you.

YOU WILL NEED

2 litre (⅓ gallon) paint can
paint stripper (optional)
sandpaper
card (cardboard)
scissors
felt-tipped pen
drill, with size 6 twist metal bit
hammer and nail (optional)
metal file
pendant lamp fitting
matt (flat) black emulsion (latex) paint
paintbrush
4 litre (¾ gallon) paint can
string
pipe-bending spring
2.75m (3yds) copper pipe
hacksaw
rubber grommets
silver sand to fill larger can

one *Strip off the paint or remove the label from the smaller can, then rub down the surface with sandpaper. This will be the shade. Cut a strip of card (cardboard) the height of the can, then mark off three equal sections. Mark the other side in the same way but so that the marks fall halfway between the others. Use the strip to mark the drilling points around the can.*

two *Drill holes through all the marked points. Drilling through metal is not difficult, but if the drill bit slips, dent each mark slightly with a hammer and nail before drilling. Find the centre of the base of the can·and drill four or five holes close together to make a larger hole. Use the end of a metal file to turn this into an even, circular hole that is the right size for a pendant lamp fitting.*

three *Roughen up the outside of the can with a file, smoothing the drilled-hole edges and scratching a texture into the surface. Paint the outside of the larger paint can matt (flat) black. Paint the lid separately. Drill a hole for the cord near the base of the can. The pipe-bending spring will not be as long as the copper pipe, so attach a piece of string to one end of the spring. Mark the string at intervals so that you will be able to tell how far down the copper pipe the string is.*

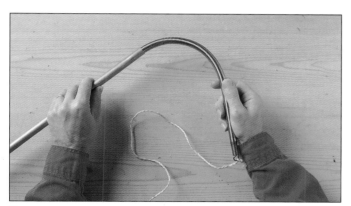

four *Insert the spring into the pipe and start to shape the top third of the pipe into a semi-circle. You will not be able to bend the pipe in one go, so make small bends, bringing the spring back up the pipe as you work. You will not be able to bend the very end of the pipe, so saw off the straight section so that the shade will hang at the end of the curve. Then fix the rubber grommet to the end of the copper pipe.*

five *At this stage you need an electrician to thread the flex through the copper pipe and wire the fitting to it. The two halves of the fitting hold the shade between them. Drill a centrally positioned hole in the lid of the large can to take the copper pipe. Fit the lid over the base of the pipe and feed the flex out through the hole drilled near the base. Hold the lamp upright in the can and fill it with sand to ensure stability. Push the lid firmly on to the can.*

INCA BIRD PRINT LAMP

MAKE AN IMPRESSION on a tall conical lampshade by stamping it all over with a strong printed pattern. The shade used here is made of thin, mottled cardboard that resembles vellum in appearance and which casts a warm glow when the lamp is lit. The stamp is based on an Inca bird design that is bold enough for a beginner to cut and is even enhanced by a slightly rough cutting style.

YOU WILL NEED

white paper

spray adhesive

high-density foam

scalpel

PVA (white) glue

flat plate

ready-made wallpaper paste

golden brown and darker brown ready-mixed watercolour paint in droppered bottle

small paint roller

conical paper lampshade

one *Photocopy the motif from the template at the back of the book. Spray the back of the copy lightly with adhesive and stick it on to the foam block. Cut around the shape with the scalpel and scoop away the back-ground so that the motif stands proud.*

two *Put about a dessertspoonful of the glue on to the plate. Add a similar amount of wallpaper paste and a few drops of golden brown paint and mix well. Run the roller through the mixture to coat it evenly and use it to coat the stamp.*

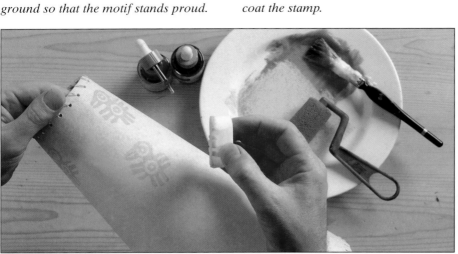

three *Print the bird motif on the lampshade by pressing the stamp on to the surface and then removing it directly. The wallpaper paste makes the paint gelatinous, leaving an interesting texture when you lift the stamp.*

four *Add a few drops of the darker paint to the mixture and stamp more motifs on the shade.*

Woody NIGHTSHADE

WOOD VENEER IS A THIN SHEET shaved from a seasoned tree trunk and is sold by timber merchants who supply furniture makers. Each sheet is unique, so choose the veneer with the best grain; it will look even better with light shining through it. The lampshade shown here is made from flamed-ash veneer. The veneer hangs from a simple wooden frame but you could use a square picture frame (without the glass). Carefully remove one edge of the frame, thread on the curtain rings and glue the piece back. Suspend the veneer from the frame using clipped curtain rings. Hang the lampshade on leather thongs or cord from a ceiling hook, with a pendant lamp fitting and bulb dangling inside it.

YOU WILL NEED

4 equal lengths of wooden dowel, mitred

glue gun with all-purpose glue sticks

curtain rings with clip attachments

metal ruler

scalpel

sheet of wood veneer

4 equal lengths of cord or leather thongs

one *Join three pieces of dowel using the glue gun. Thread the curtain rings on to the frame before gluing the last piece of dowel in place.*

two *Measure the width of one side of the frame and, using the scalpel, cut four strips of veneer, one for each side. Make the length roughly twice the width; for a natural look the pieces should not be precisely the same size.*

three *To finish, attach two clips to each sheet of veneer, then tie a cord or thong to each corner for hanging.*

ECCENTRIC CREPE LIGHT

CREPE (PAPER) BANDAGE IS GREAT material to work with and makes a fun lampshade. It has just enough stretch for a good tight fit and the textured surface clings to itself as you layer the bandage. Keep an even tension as you wind it around a wire frame and use hot glue at key points, if necessary, to prevent any slipping or sagging. Make sure you leave an opening at the top, however, to allow the hot air to escape.

YOU WILL NEED

copper bonsai-training wire

wire-cutters

long-nosed (needlenose) pliers

thinner wire

glue gun with all-purpose glue sticks

rolls of bandage

one *Cut three equal lengths of bonsai-training wire and bend each into three curves, using the pliers. The wire will straighten up when you release it, so exaggerate the shapes as you bend them.*

two *Bind the three ends of the bonsai wire firmly with the thinner wire. Be generous with the amount of wire because you need to make a solid fixture. Use the long-nosed (needle-nose) pliers to help you bind tightly.*

three *Run another length of wire between the three struts, winding it tightly around each strut, to form the lowest of three enclosing wires that will later provide the framework for the bandage binding.*

four *Wind round two more lengths of wire to complete the frame. Twist the ends of the struts into curved "feet".*

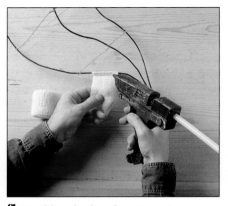

five *Glue the bandage to a strut about 5cm (2in) from the binding at the top. Wrap tightly to fix firmly. Wrap the bandage around the frame, pulling it to get the tension right. Apply glue whenever it crosses a strut.*

six *Wrap and glue a small length of bandage to cover the wire binding right at the top of the framework. Use the glue gun to seal the edge and be sure to leave a 5cm (2in) gap around the top in order for the heat to escape.*

RAFFIA STANDARD LAMP

STANDARD LAMPS PROVIDE the perfect overhead light to read by without killing the atmosphere of a room as bright central ceiling lights often do. Placing one in the corner means that an individual can see what he or she is doing, while the rest of the room can be dimmed for watching television or general relaxation. Here, a turned-wood standard lamp has been enclosed in a sheath of raffia that is finished off by a "thatched" base that resembles a very clean chimney-sweep's brush.

YOU WILL NEED

turned-wood standard lamp
rubber bands
several bunches of
natural-coloured raffia
scissors
coloured raffia

one *Place a rubber band at the bottom of the pole. Unravel the raffia and cut a handful of 38cm (15in) lengths. Fold the lengths in half and tuck them under the band, so that it holds them in place just below the fold. Continue inserting folded lengths until the base is completely covered.*

two *Wind a strand of raffia around the rubber band several times and tie it tightly to hold the raffia base in place.*

three *Place a rubber band around the top of the lamp. Tuck bunches of raffia under it until the pole is covered. About 25cm (10in) down from the band, wind a strand of raffia around the pole. Continue at intervals.*

four *At the base, tuck the raffia into the top of the base raffia, then bind to cover the join. Trim any loose ends. Cover the plain raffia bindings with coloured raffia.*

LIME-WASHED LAMP BASE

ONE OF THE MOST effective ways of updating a dull lamp is to give the base a fashionable paint finish and add a fresh new shade. Look out for bargains in second-hand stores and at flea markets, then give them new life with a special paint treatment. This turned-wood lamp base has been given a limed look by applying and rubbing back two colours. The first blue-grey coat of paint is rubbed off but remains in the grain and the grooves. The second coat of white paint is also rubbed back, leaving a transparent, lime-washed look.

YOU WILL NEED

plain turned-wood
lamp base

fine-grade sandpaper

emulsion (latex) paint in
blue-grey and white

paintbrushes

2 cloths

one *Remove any surface finish on the base and sand it to a smooth finish. Then paint the bare wood with a coat of blue-grey paint.*

two *Before the paint has dried, rub it off with a cloth, leaving some colour in the grooves and grain. Allow to dry.*

three *Gently rub the decorative, raised parts of the lamp base with fine-grade sandpaper.*

four *Paint the whole lamp base with white paint. Rub off the paint before it has dried, using another cloth, and then allow to dry. Gently sand the decorative raised parts to create the lime-washed look.*

TRIPOD LIGHT

THIS CONTEMPORARY-LOOKING standard lamp appears quite delicate, but the tripod legs are very stable. The simple design makes it ideal for a Japanese-style room, particularly if a plain shade is fitted. The base consists of three pieces of wooden dowel fitted into angled holes drilled in a circle of wood. The frame of the shade is covered with butter muslin. The lamp is assembled by screwing a lamp fitting to the wooden disc, over a central hole through which the flex passes.

YOU WILL NEED

dark oak wood stain

3 x 1m (1yd) lengths of wooden dowel

soft cloth

pencil

pair of compasses

square piece of wood

clamp

2 scraps of wood

coping saw

drill, with twist bit

craft knife or scalpel

wood glue

tape measure

large cylindrical shade frame

dressmaker's scissors

2.75m (3yds) unbleached butter-coloured muslin

dressmaker's pins

rust-coloured 4-ply wool

darning needle

shade carrier

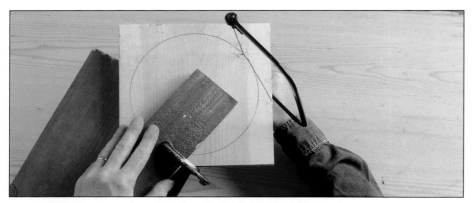

one *Rub the wood stain into the dowel with the cloth. Draw a circle with an 18cm (7in) diameter on the square of wood, then clamp it ready for sawing. Protect it from the clamp with scraps of wood. Saw in from the edge at an angle and follow the curve with the blade. Move the wood around so that you can saw comfortably.*

two *Using a drill bit that is marginally narrower than the dowel, drill three angled holes through the wood circle. To do this, hold the drill directly above the centre, then tilt it slightly towards the edge; the angle will then be correct.*

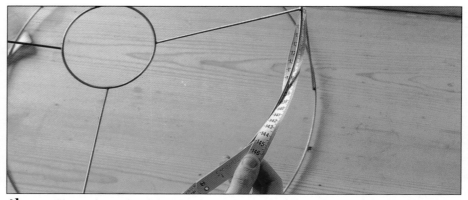

three *Shave the ends of the lengths of dowel slightly with a craft knife or scalpel, apply wood glue and then push them into the drilled holes. Apply glue to the lengths of dowel where they intersect. Allow to dry. To cover the frame, measure around the circumference and height. Cut a double thickness of muslin 10cm (4in) wider than the height of the shade and long enough to fit around it, with an extra 4cm (1½in) as a seam allowance. Pin one end of the muslin along a strut, leaving 2cm (¾in) at each end for a seam, and gathering the fabric slightly as you go.*

four *Pin the muslin along the next strut and sew in place using blanket stitch. To sew blanket stitch, insert the needle behind the strut and pull it out in front. Do not pull the wool through. Take the needle through the loop of wool, then pull the wool tight. Continue stitching the muslin to each strut in the same way until you reach the first pinned seam. When you reach the final strut, join the two edges and stitch them together, still using blanket stitch.*

five *Finish off the top and bottom by rolling the edges around the wire frame, then pin and stitch them in place. Ask an electrician to attach the light fittings to the tripod, then place the shade on the carrier.*

PRIMARY PLASTIC

THIN SHEETS OF OPAQUE, coloured plastic, which are available from art supply shops, make excellent lampshade materials. They are available in a range of colours, and the edges can be cut decoratively, with no need for seaming, and fastened in place with nuts and bolts. As plastic is a fairly rigid material, it does not require a supporting frame although you can use one for a template if you wish.

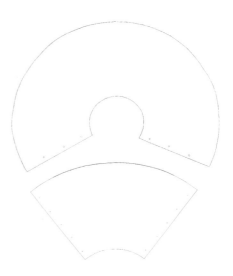

RED SHADE

one *Enlarge the template at the back of the book and transfer it on to brown paper. Spray the back with adhesive and stick it on to the red sheet. Cut out the shade with a craft knife. Make a card template for the sawtooth pattern. Place it on the edge of the brown-paper pattern, on the plastic sheet, and draw round it to create a zigzag.*

two *Cut out the sawtooth border. Cut towards the outside edge every time. Remove the paper and fix the long edges of the shade together with cloth tape. Place a strip of masking tape along this seam. Place the wood block behind the seam, then drill three holes through the plastic. Remove the tape and screw in the nuts and bolts.*

YELLOW SHADE

one *Enlarge the template at the back of the book and transfer it to brown paper. Spray the back with adhesive and stick it on to a sheet of yellow plastic. Place on the cutting mat and cut out the shade using a craft knife.*

two *Overlap the two long edges of the shade and secure with a strip of cloth tape. Then place a strip of masking tape along this seam.*

three *Using a ruler, mark five equal divisions along the seam. Place a wooden block behind the seam and carefully drill a hole through the plastic at each mark. Start peeling off the tape at the top of the shade and screw in a nut and bolt each time a drilled hole is exposed.*

TEMPLATES

The templates may be resized to any scale required. They can be enlarged or reduced using a photocopier.

Scandinavian Room
page 40

Santa Fe Walls
page 30

Inca Bird Print
page 80

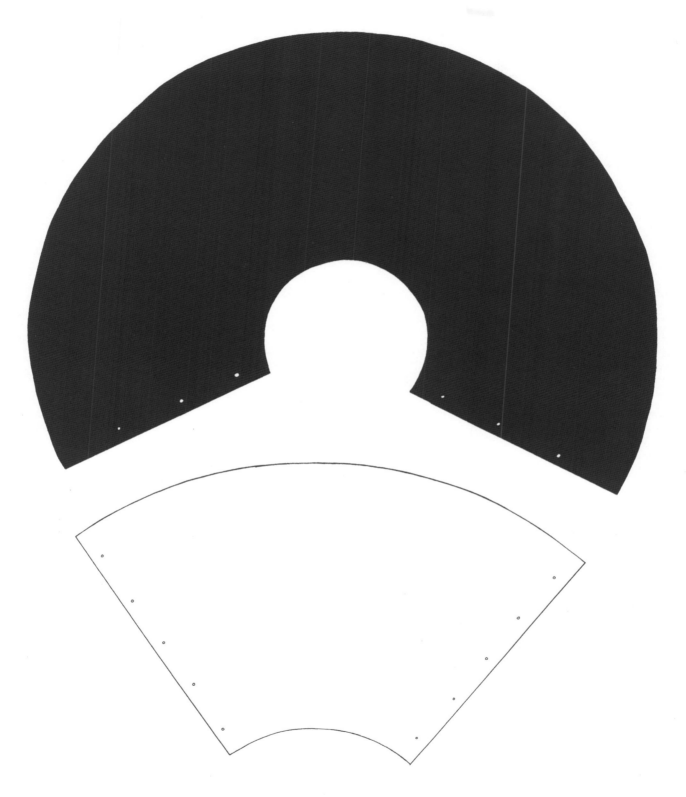

Primary Plastic
page 92

ᴵNDEX